A tool for planning your ministry around Christ's mission

Mission Minded

by Peter Bolt

matthiasmedia

Mission Minded
First published, 1992

Matthias Media
(St Matthias Press Ltd. ACN 067 558 365)
PO Box 225
Kingsford NSW 2032
Australia
Telephone: (02) 9663 1478; international: +61-2-9663-1478
Facsimile: (02) 9663 3265; international: +61-2-9663-3265
Email: info@matthiasmedia.com.au
Internet: www.matthiasmedia.com.au

ISBN 1 876326 20 4

Cover design and typesetting by Lankshear Design Pty Ltd.

Contents

How to use this book

This book is for anyone in ministry, which means it is really for all Christians, since all of us have an obligation to serve others. It contains a simple planning tool which can be used to think about what we're currently doing, what we ought to be doing and how to go about it.

Individuals

If you're working through this book on your own to apply it to your own particular ministry, you should find it fairly straightforward. Each chapter (from chapter 2 onwards) shows you a different way to focus your ministry on Christ's mission. You could either:

- work through each of the suggestions as you go, pausing after each chapter to do your own thinking and planning; or
- read the whole book through quickly to get an idea of how it all works and then come back and work through each phase more slowly.

Groups

The tool is also extremely valuable for groups, such as church committees, parish councils, leadership teams, and so on. You could work through the chapters at a series of regular meetings, or you could go away together for a few days and do it intensively. The best method would probably be to read each chapter privately, in advance, and then get together to discuss its content and to work through the implications for your ministry.

Chapter 1

Mission or Maintenance?

Are you involved in Mission or Maintenance? What a question! How do you know? And who wants to answer it anyway? The way the question is often put makes it clear that you take a risk if you answer it. Your answer will firmly place you in only one of two groups—it will place you amongst the real movers who are going somewhere and taking their group of Christians with them, or it will reveal that you are part of the vast mass of Christian leaders who have supposedly renounced that title in practice, are going nowhere and taking no-one with them! So what does the question do for you? Does it bring on cold sweats, as you feel your whole life and ministry and self-esteem threatened? Or does it give you a touch of Pharisaic pride, seeing that you know you are on the right track and can revel in the answer you have been invited to spruik about?

These two M-words seem to have become a new dividing stick amongst Christians, and a new way to evaluate a minister's work. Recently I heard of one group of people on the prowl for a new pastor who bewailed the fact that 95% of the people they interviewed were in 'Maintenance Mode' not 'Mission Mode'. It sounds like two competing Christian fashion magazines, doesn't it? This group were after a 'Mission Minded' not 'Maintenance Minded' pastor, and so they hadn't, at that time, found someone for their charge. We can only speculate about the 95% they left behind: did this group of concerned pastor-seekers inform the rejected clergy of their ailment, and what happened when they did? Were the Maintenance men hard-liners who had chosen to be 'Self-consciously Maintenance Minded', were proud of it, and glad to see the backs of these Mission Seeking Morons! Or were they 'Accidentally Maintenance Minded', somehow not noticing that they had left their Mission behind until this group of nouveau Pharisees kindly informed them that they hadn't met the standards of this new law? Or were they 'Occasionally Maintenance Minded', vacillating between moments of Mission and moments of Maintenance, and unfortunately happened to be wallowing in the latter when they were visited by the 'Mission Mafia'? Were they left in their offices wondering where they went wrong?

Of course, there *is* a point to the distinction, even if it shouldn't be used against fellow Christians for whom Christ died. Every Christian is drafted into Christ's Mission as soon as they are converted. The Son of Man came to seek and to save the lost (Lk 19:10), and on this side of his death and resurrection his people are to carry on this task until he returns. To follow Jesus as his disciple means to be unashamed of him *and his words*, being prepared to suffer for his sake *and for the sake of his gospel* (Mk 8:35, 38). Because we have believed this marvelous gospel, we will speak about its good news (2 Cor 4:13–14; see also 1 Thess 1). It is a usual reaction for converted people to want to "proclaim the excellencies of him who called you out of darkness into his marvellous light" (1 Pet 2:9), and as soon as you open your mouth you step into the Mission. Mission is clearly the priority for individual Christians, and for groups of Christians, for it is the priority of our Lord and our God.

Then there is Maintenance. In the Mafia's vocabulary this is clearly on the down-side. They mean by this term 'simply maintaining the status quo', long after the reason for that 'quo' has been lost or outdated or forgotten or brutally murdered. So whatever gets started keeps going on and on and on and on. Nothing ever changes; this year is the same as last year, and the year before that. The only reason for doing anything is that 'We've always done it that way'. The only reason needed to *not* do something is that 'We've never done it that way'. This kind of Maintenance smells very much like the traditions of men that get in the way of the real things of God's Kingdom (Mk 7:5-8), and it sounds very close to the man-made religious practices that God hated in the Old Testament and that Jesus and the apostles attacked in the New. What Christian wants that? And what Christian leader wants to be leading in that direction? Such Maintenance is rightly despised.

But the confusing thing is that there is a right kind of Maintenance. Isn't it right to nurture people's faith, maintain their Christian walk, help them to offer their whole lives in worship of their God, keep them persevering to the end, and all that? Don't some of the things already going on in the church help maintain such good directions? Why should they be changed just to avoid the slanders of the Mission Mafia? Of course there is a place for maintaining the status quo—as long as the status quo still serves a useful purpose in furthering Christ's Mission to a lost world. That is the key.

Another problem is that we can all get in a rut. Despite good intentions and commitments to stay in 'Mission Mode', the pressures and busyness of normal twenty-first century life combined with the pressures and busyness of normal twenty-first century Christian ministry, seem to drag us towards a 'Maintenance Mentality'. It is far easier to stay with what we've got. And it is just plain hard work to get something new up and running. It is a breeze to do whatever others thrust upon you, but a stormy process indeed to think of what you would like to thrust upon them. It makes you so acceptable to others when you respond to their needs, rather than saying 'No' to them so you can pursue your own agenda on their behalf. Scratching people where they say they have an itch pleases everyone—everyone, that is, except that confounded Mission Mafia! They persist in shaking their heads in your direction and whispering to each other behind their hands.

To save face with this group, what can we do? But the issue is more important than that, isn't it? To help overcome the natural drag away from Mission, what can we do? For Christ's Mission is about saving the lost. Without Christ, people are utterly lost. With Christ they are utterly found; they are utterly saved. It is therefore of the utmost importance to be involved in his Mission, and to maintain only those things that further his Mission. The question is, how can we do it?

▸ *Mission Goals*. Part of the answer involves setting goals. But we can set goals about anything and everything—just setting goals is not the thing. Our goals ought to be *Mission* goals, and these Mission goals ought then to govern our ministry. That *doesn't* mean that there will be no Maintenance, but it *does* mean that Maintenance will be justified according to the Mission goals, like anything else that gets a guernsey in our ministry.

► *Biblical.* Mission goals will consist of some fairly general things that will always be a part of any Christian ministry, for these things are determined by the Bible. People will always need to be evangelized; Christians will always need to be edified in their faith and equipped for Christian service (Eph 4:12); faithful people will always need to be freed up to teach other faithful people to teach other faithful people to... (2 Tim 2:2).

► *Contextual.* Such general and necessary goals may take different specific forms in various places and at various times, or to various types of people. In other words, our biblical goals might then be applied to our own particular historical and social context in the real world. But no matter what specific form they may take, they are plainly drawn from God's Word and should therefore govern everything else.

What follows is a simple tool. It is not 'Everything you wanted to know about ministry, but were afraid to ask'. It will not give you all the answers to becoming Mission Minded about ministry—I hope I'm not that big-headed. It will also need further refinement from you as you use it in the specific context of your ministry. But it is a tool that will help you think through your ministry in a way that is governed by Mission goals.

It is a tool that will be useful to anyone engaged in Christian ministry. And that means you—for all Christians are involved in ministry (Eph 4:12). It is helpful for:

- ministry one-to-one
- churches setting up new ministries
- churches analysing their old ministries
- anyone with some leadership role in a structured ministry situation such as a Sunday School Class, a youth group or an Adult Bible Study
- a pastor who has oversight of all the ministries in a church

Without further ado, let's take a look at it. Who knows, you may have it mastered before the Mission Mafia next comes knocking on your door!

Chapter 2

Aiming at something biblical

The tool to help resurrect us from Maintenance to that far more acceptable 'M' is extremely simple. It has to be, right? Who wants something that is so complex that no-one even knows which way is up?

The tool consists of a piece of paper. That's right, an ordinary piece of paper—any colour, practically any size, and it doesn't matter if it has a Bible verse along the bottom or not. Along the top of the paper are listed several very general goals that are drawn from the Bible. Several? Okay, basically it is only two, but they are subdivided so that the tool doesn't look too basic (we have our pride, don't we?). Two? Well, there is also an additional 'supportive goal' which I'll mention later. Under these goals we have columns drawn and, to the far left, we have a column that is blank for the moment. In the following chapters we will discover that the contents of this left-hand column are variable, depending upon how the tool is being applied. Here is a diagram, so that we are all picturing the same thing right at the beginning:

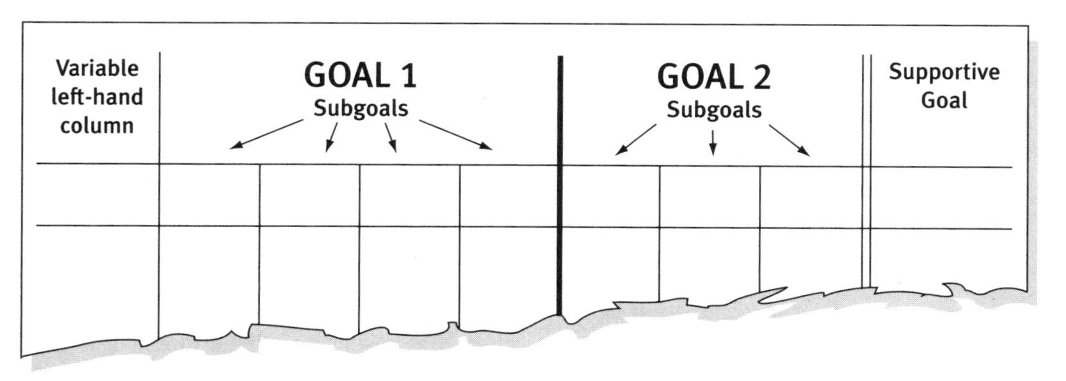

There are two goals that every Christian involved in ministry ought to adopt. These general goals form the basis of this mission tool.

1. Evangelism

The first is evangelism. Here I am talking about taking the gospel to unbelievers. God's chosen way of bringing people into his Kingdom is through the proclamation of the gospel of Christ. As men and women hear of Christ's death and resurrection on their behalf, and his present reign as Lord before his promised return, and they believe, so they enter into God's Kingdom. Such people then experience the joy of forgiveness of sins, the certainty of eternal life, and the freedom of Christian discipleship in fellowship with other believers. But the entry point is the proclamation of the gospel. Whenever the gospel is proclaimed, that is evangelism.

Now, it is certainly true that we never outgrow our need for the gospel of Jesus Christ. It is how we become Christians, and it is how we continue as Christians too (see Colossians 2:6–7). So, in this sense, we always need to be 'evangelised', for we always need to hear that gospel again. But, for the sake of our tool, we can talk of evangelism in a narrower sense. What I am getting at with this first goal can be called 'Primary evangelism', that is, telling the gospel to someone who is not yet a believer. Sometimes it is also called 'Outreach', for it is proclaiming the gospel of Christ, reaching out to the non-Christian world in the hope that they might be saved.

Now, if it is true that evangelism is the proclamation of the gospel, part of our Mission goals must be that Jesus' name is proclaimed as the only way of salvation. "Salvation is found in no-one else, for there is no other name under heaven given to men by which we must be saved" (Acts 4:12). In another place, Paul says: "For how can they call on the one in whom they have not believed? And how can they believe in the one of whom they have not heard? And how can they hear without someone preaching to them? And how can they preach unless they are sent?" (Rom 10:14-15). When he says this, he is making the point that Israel in fact *received* the necessary preaching and still refused to believe. But, for our purposes, we simply need to notice the logical questions that he asks in the course of his argument. Evangelism is necessary for anyone to hear about Jesus and so believe and be saved. Evangelism is the proclamation of the gospel. This proclamation needs to be done by somebody.

Before a person can hear the gospel they need to be in contact with a gospel preacher, that is, a Christian. It is God's chosen method that he sends preachers of the gospel to others. I guess he could have done it some other way if he had chosen to do so, but the fact is, he didn't. Evangelism is done by people to people for people. This then gives us a sub-goal: there must be contact between the Christian (the gospel preacher) and the one who needs to hear the gospel. Christians need to be in contact with people so that they can take the opportunities that God will provide for gospel proclamation.

Now, a lot of people cross our path in the course of normal life: neighbours, workmates, family and friends; other people's neighbours, workmates, family, and friends; visitors to church, casual acquaintances, etc. These people have contact with a Christian by virtue of these relationships. But there are other people who never come into contact with a Christian in the normal course of life. How can these people hear the gospel? Surely they must somehow be reached as well. This gives us another sub-goal: We ought to attempt to raise people's awareness of the gospel or Christians or our church, in the hope of making contact with them in the future.

It also seems fairly common that people are in contact with a Christian for some time before an opportunity for evangelism is taken by the Christian. This period of time can be called 'pre-evangelism'. Certainly the Christian ought to be praying for opportunities to share the gospel so that the relationship is heading towards evangelism. However, until the gospel is actually proclaimed it is not evangelism, just pre-evangelism.

At this point I need to deal with a potential confusion. Those of you who are 'on the ball' will notice that the Big Goal is 'Evangelism', and the fourth sub-goal is also 'Evangelism'. If you are someone who is up on how headings usually work, you may think that this indicates that all four things could be called 'Evangelism'. Don't get confused here, but I am trying to show something else. 'Evangelism' in the Bible is the activity of proclaiming the gospel. If the gospel is not proclaimed, then, technically speaking, no evangelism has taken place either. This means that the first three sub-goals are NOT (technically speaking) evangelism in their own right.

What the diagram tries to show is that it is useful to think about the various stages that a person *may* go through (they don't *always* have to go through them!) in the process of being converted. In other words, the first three sub-goals are all heading towards the main goal of evangelism proper!

So, under our first main goal of Evangelism, we have ended up with four sub-goals, all heading towards the proclamation of the gospel to a non-Christian. These can be set out as follows, with an arrow to indicate the desired direction of movement:

Variable left-hand column	GOAL 1 = EVANGELISM				GOAL 2
	Raising Awareness	Initial Contact	Pre-Evangelism	Evangelism	
	→	→	→	→	

2. Edification

The second major goal is edification. Here I am talking about taking the gospel to those who are believers already.

Edification means 'building' (just like we sometimes call a building an 'edifice'—although, admittedly, we usually reserve this term for not a very beautiful building!). When we talk of 'Edification', what are we building?

Just after Jesus was recognized as the Messiah by his disciples, he announced to them: "I will build my church" (Matt 16:18). In the Old Testament, Israel had gathered around Mt Sinai, as God's church, God's assembly. Jesus told his disciples that he has a church to build. He will gather his people around himself. One day, in heaven, this gathering will be complete, with people from all nations and languages gathered around Jesus (see Rev 4–5).

In the meantime, Jesus is building his church. He builds it by gathering people around him now, through the gospel. As people believe the gospel, and put their trust in Jesus as Lord, so they become part of his assembly, his church. As they gather together to hear God's word, they express the reality that will be true forever in heaven, they are Christ's people (see Heb. 10:24–25; 12:22-24).

He also builds his church by bringing it towards the maturity it will have in heaven. God wants all of his people to be conformed more and more to the likeness of Jesus Christ. Edification is building towards this goal. It involves Christians growing into his likeness. Of course, this will only be completed on the Last Day, but it is the present aim of every Christian's life to progress towards the maturity that will be theirs on that Last Day.

This goal of Edification can also be broken down into sub-goals. When people are first converted to Christ, it is always beneficial to give them some special treatment, some basic 'follow-up'. It seems that the apostle Paul was keen to do this with the Thessalonians, since he writes to them and also sends Timothy to find out about their faith (1 Thess 3:1-5). In fact, a good case can be made that it was his constant practice to 'follow-up' new believers.

But the need for edification never stops, for when it ceases we will have arrived in heaven. (And does it stop there? I'll wait and see!) Until that day, all Christians need to be 'nurtured' in their Christian life.

Two further sub-goals can now be added to the tool:

Variable left-hand column	EVANGELISM				EDIFICATION			Supportive Goal
	Raising Awareness	Initial Contact	Pre-Evangelism	Evangelism	Follow-up	Nurture		

But there is more to the Christian life than being followed-up and nurtured. If that was all, we would not be too different from the Pharisees who were so scrupulously concerned about their own piety. This self-centred religion may be the natural default state of every human heart, but Christ's followers know that this is not true religion. Christ, in his mercy, has given each Christian the 'work of service', or ministry, to be engaged in for the sake of his body, the church (Eph 4:11-12). His aim in doing so was that the church might be built (edified). This happens both individually and together. It is not just individual Christians who need to be built towards maturity, but the whole of Christ's church. His purposes are far wider than this individual or that individual; he is creating a whole new people for himself. And it is as "...each part does its work" that the "...whole body...grows and builds itself up in love" (Eph 4:16).

Within Christ's church, some people have a special kind of ministry. Those people who bring God's word to the rest of the church have been given to the church so that all ministries will be developed and nurtured. "(Christ) gave some to be apostles, some to be prophets, some to be evangelists, and some as pastors/teachers, to prepare God's people for the work of service, so that the body of Christ may be built up" (Eph 4:11-12). These people are to train and equip Christians, by the explanation of God's word, for the work of service (their 'ministries').

This enables another sub-goal to be formulated. As soon as you have Christians, you have people who ought to be engaged in and trained for ministry for the greater benefit of Christ's body, the church. Therefore we ought to aim at training Christians for ministry. Our tool is now getting wider:

Variable left-hand column	EVANGELISM				EDIFICATION			Supportive Goal
	Raising Awareness	Initial Contact	Pre-Evangelism	Evangelism	Follow-up	Nurture	Training in Ministry	

3. Support to Ministry

There is one more goal to be added to our basic tool. The double line indicates that it is in its own category, which we can call 'support to ministry'. Here I am talking about practical, 'behind the scenes' support work to facilitate taking the gospel to unbelievers (Evangelism), and to believers (Edification).

Now, I know that whatever ministry a Christian is involved in could be called ministry in the full sense. But it will be seen below that it is useful to separate 'frontline ministry'—i.e. the activities that have some specific and direct role in either getting the gospel to people or growing the church—and those activities that *support* this ministry. Perhaps this category is close to what the Bible calls the gift of administration or 'helps' (1 Cor 12:28). This category will be further clarified when examples are given in Chapter 7.

The basic tool has now been constructed. To enable us to set Mission goals for our ministry, certain general goals can be drawn from the Bible and slightly sub-divided to give us the following:

Variable left-hand column	EVANGELISM				EDIFICATION			SUPPORT TO MINISTRY
	Raising Awareness	Initial Contact	Pre-Evangelism	Evangelism	Follow-up	Nurture	Training in Ministry	Support to Ministry

4. Summary of Tool

It may be helpful at this point to summarize the definitions of each of these sub-goals:

Variable left-hand column	EVANGELISM				EDIFICATION			SUPPORT TO MINISTRY
	Raising Awareness	Initial Contact	Pre-Evangelism	Evangelism	Follow-up	Nurture	Training in Ministry	Support to Ministry
	No *personal* contact	A real person is contacted	A relationship-builder, no gospel shared	Gospel is shared	First help after becoming a Christian	Ongoing help in being a Christian	Help in helping others	'Behind the scenes' work that assists everything else

Now that the goals and subgoals are listed across our page, we are almost ready to turn to the most important left-hand variable column. But before we do, let's take a look at these goals again. As we do so, it becomes apparent that there is a progression from left to right. Take Mr. Average Unbeliever. He starts out totally unaware that anything Christian even exists. He thinks churches are just ornate old buildings, or poor-quality meeting halls for strange practices he has no particular interest in. He thinks being religious means never ever missing the Friday after-work session at the pub. What does he need? He needs Column One: he needs to have his awareness of Christianity raised.

Then he may come across a Christian. Column Two has been filled: Initial Contact.

Say he then gets to know this Christian for some time—Column Three: Pre-evangelism.

Then, eventually, the Christian (who has been praying for opportunities to share the gospel with Mr Average) asks him if he knows anything about Jesus Christ and eternal life and all that stuff. He doesn't, so the Christian asks whether he'd mind if he let him have it. He doesn't, so he does—Column Four: Evangelism.

Mr Average reckons it is the best news he's heard since last year's Christmas bonus, so he believes it and becomes a Christian. His new brother, a truly amazing specimen, decides to meet with him weekly to help him understand the new life he has just received—Column Five: Follow-Up.

Lo and behold, Mr Average-Ex-Unbeliever begins at church and Bible study—Column Six: Nurture.

After a while he wants to learn how to share the gospel with others who are still like he used to be, so he joins a Personal Evangelism course at the local church hall—Column Seven: Training in Ministry.

And sometime during the whole process he realises that he can give some of his money to enable other people to hear the good news that he has heard—Column Eight: Support to Ministry.

Of course, not everyone moves through all these stages, and it certainly isn't strictly chronological. In fact, many things may be going on at the same time and people may cross from one column to the next without any show of emotion whatsoever! But we can still say that there is a loose progression from left to right on the page—well, at least to the double line, for it marks that separate category (see chapter 7).

Now that we have the top of the page all set up, what happens down the left-hand side?

Chapter 3

The left-handed game: analysis

The left-hand column varies according to how the tool is used. The following chapters will outline these uses by suggesting various left-hand columns.

Since we have all but admitted that we are already engaged in ministry but probably in Maintenance Mode (at least sometimes, if only because we really don't know how to recognize this problem), why don't we begin with what we've already got. To use that expression that has become a cliché, let's use the tool to see *where we are coming from*. The tool is extremely useful for *analysis*.

For example, let's say you are a pastor who arrives in a church knowing very little about it (as distinct from a pastor who *leaves* a church knowing very little about it!). Changing clichés slightly, you want to assess *where the church is at*. Get out your paper, draw up the goals and their underlying columns and leave your hand poised over the vacant left-hand column. If it makes you feel like you are getting somewhere you can even write at its head 'Analysis', or 'St Bob's' plus the date, or even 'Analysis of St Bob's as at' plus the date, if you want to be absolutely precise-verging-on-overkill.

► *List Activities.* Then, on a new line each time, list out totally at random all the activities that you know the church is involved in. List everything and anything, no matter how big or small. You ought to get a page like the one on page 20 (only with your church's activities on it).

ANALYSIS OF ST BOB'S

ACTIVITY	EVANGELISM				EDIFICATION		
	Raising Awareness	Initial Contact	Pre-Evangelism	Evangelism	Follow-up	Nurture	Training in Ministry
Sunday Church							
Simply Christianity							
C E Follow-up							
Craft groups							
Bible study							
Playgroups							
Sunday School							
Scripture							
Youth groups							
Creche							
Baptismal visits							
Doorknocking							
Hiring ministry trainee							
Bookstall							
Golf day							
Marriages							
Funerals							
Family Sundays							
Lord's Supper							
Leafletting							
Hospitality							
Ushers							
Welcoming							
Ladies coffee morning							
Working bee							
Committee							
Rosters							
Minister							
Prayer meeting							
Morning tea							

► *Major Function?* For your next step, think about each activity in turn. Ask yourself: What is the major function of this activity, in terms of the goals and sub-goals at the top of the page?

If you have stepped beyond the exercise of a role play and you are analysing a real church, then it may even be helpful to talk to the people involved in the activity to gain their perception of what they think they are trying to achieve by their group/activity. There may be a discrepancy between what people involved perceive the function to be, and what *you* feel it ought to be, but this process should enable clarification of the goal of the activity, as well as analysis for its own sake! Another use for the tool: better communication!

► *When the goal is clear.* Once the goal is absolutely clear to you (and even to all concerned), then you can indicate this on the chart by putting a dark box in the relevant column. So, for example, you may discover that the annual 'Guest Service' is not simply so you can have a guest speaker to give you (remember, you are imagining that you are the pastor) a day off, but that it is designed for congregation members to bring their own guests to hear the gospel explained, and to be invited to make a decision to follow Christ and be saved. In other words, it falls under the main aim Evangelism. Your table will therefore look like this:

	EVANGELISM				EDIFICATION		
ACTIVITY	Raising Awareness	Initial Contact	Pre-Evangelism	Evangelism	Follow-up	Nurture	Training in Ministry
Guest Service				■			

► *When the goal is not so clear.* However, some activities may not be this simple to categorise. You may find that some activities have a number of functions, or the people involved in them may not agree on what the main function is meant to be. Well, at this stage it doesn't matter too much, for you are still analysing what you *have* got, rather than planning what you *should* get. Later on you may want to clarify or change the main function, but for the time being use dotted lines for what you perceive to be secondary functions, still trying to identify a main function with a dark box.

An example will help. A lady in the church has a monthly meeting in her home to which she invites her neighbours for coffee and some other activity. The other activity is usually something that is relevant for the type of person in the area, e.g. a talk on child rearing, a cooking demonstration, a craft thing, etc. The woman sees that this type of activity helps her to get to know non-Christian ladies, with the hope and prayer that an opportunity to share the gospel will arise. All of this puts the activity in the 'Pre-Evangelism' column. However, you also learn that, on a couple of occasions during the year, someone is invited to talk about the gospel. For instance, last year someone spoke on the meaning of Christmas, and someone else gave a talk on Easter and answered questions about Christianity. Since these activities specifically involve the proclamation of the gospel, they are Evangelism. This means that this monthly meeting functions mainly as Pre-Evangelism, but occasionally as Evangelism, and so the diagram ends up like this:

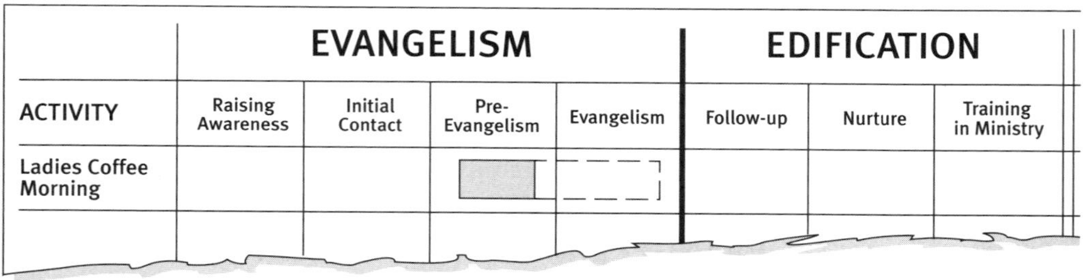

	EVANGELISM				EDIFICATION		
ACTIVITY	Raising Awareness	Initial Contact	Pre-Evangelism	Evangelism	Follow-up	Nurture	Training in Ministry
Ladies Coffee Morning			■	┄			

This process of analysis has helped to clarify that there are actually two activities going on here. The regular meeting is pre-evangelism, but the occasional special events that arise out of these meetings are actually evangelism. To be really neat, you could represent it like this:

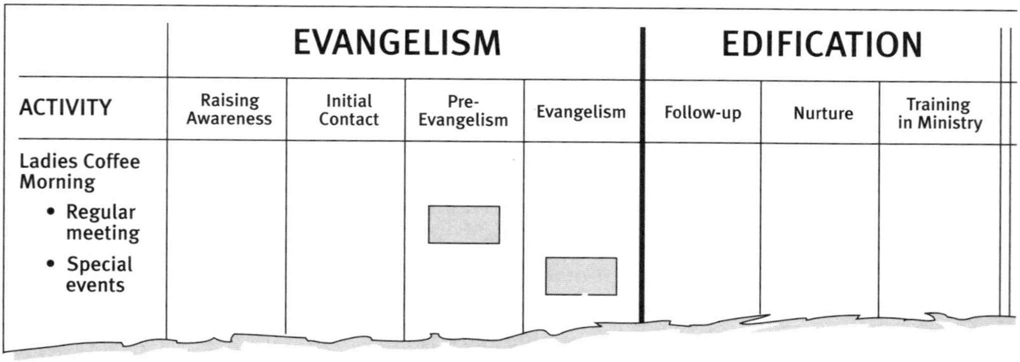

	EVANGELISM				EDIFICATION		
ACTIVITY	Raising Awareness	Initial Contact	Pre-Evangelism	Evangelism	Follow-up	Nurture	Training in Ministry
Ladies Coffee Morning							
• Regular meeting			■				
• Special events				■			

It may get even more complicated. You know an older guy who loves knocking on doors and telling people that there is a church down the road at which they would be most welcome (you have already checked, he does mean yours!) and which wants to be of any service to the community that they can be. Okay, this activity fits into 'Initial Contact'. (It isn't 'Raising Awareness' because it involves a non-Christian actually coming into personal contact with a Christian). But then, as you talk to this guy, you also find out that he loves taking someone with him on his visits, because he feels that they will benefit from the experience and be more confident about sharing their own faith some day. That means that he has the aim of training someone else for ministry. Now your diagram has a box in two columns that are not next to each other—it may not be neat, but it is certainly informative:

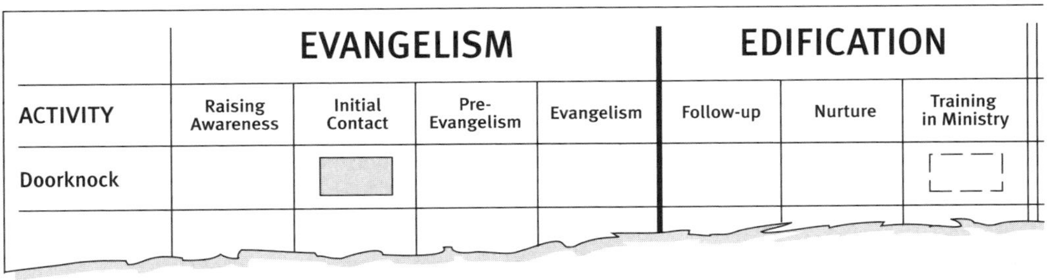

	EVANGELISM				EDIFICATION		
ACTIVITY	Raising Awareness	Initial Contact	Pre-Evangelism	Evangelism	Follow-up	Nurture	Training in Ministry
Doorknock		■					[ ]

Doing such thinking about every activity you have listed may well be hard, but it will certainly be most worthwhile. When you have finished, you will immediately see where the focus of your church lies—whether there is a spread of activities across all goals, or whether there is some imbalance.

If there are a lot of dotted lines, it means that there are a lot of activities with unclear goals and more clarification is needed. A church with the following analysis needs to work out what they are trying to achieve:

ACTIVITY	EVANGELISM				EDIFICATION		
	Raising Awareness	Initial Contact	Pre-Evangelism	Evangelism	Follow-up	Nurture	Training in Ministry
Doorknocking							
Baptismal inquiries							
Guest services							
Church							

The old proverb says that if you aim at nothing you are sure to hit it. It seems equally true that if you aim at everything you are sure to hit just as much as if you aimed at nothing! My guess is that this church would have quite a lot of furious activity that is achieving very little because, quite simply, it is aiming at too little by trying to aim at everything with every activity! Activities with a clearly defined function will be more productive in the long run.

Are there heaps of boxes in one column? Like for this church, which has an oversupply of pre-evangelistic activities:

ACTIVITY	EVANGELISM				EDIFICATION		
	Raising Awareness	Initial Contact	Pre-Evangelism	Evangelism	Follow-up	Nurture	Training in Ministry
Coffee morning							
Men's mechanics night							
Men's golf day							
Bush dance							
Carols by Candlelight							

Or maybe this one, which has plenty of food for the saints, but apparently nothing else (in my experience this diagram turns up quite commonly in churches):

	EVANGELISM				EDIFICATION		
ACTIVITY	Raising Awareness	Initial Contact	Pre-Evangelism	Evangelism	Follow-up	Nurture	Training in Ministry
Morning church							
Evening church							
Bible study							
Input day							
Correspondence Course group							

The problem with the first is that all the pre-evangelism in the world won't get anyone converted. I would guess that this church had lots of good contact with non-Christian people. I would also guess that this church would be full of good-hearted people who were run down, worn out, and rather frustrated. Pre-evangelistic events usually take a lot of time and energy to make them worthwhile and to sustain them over time. In other words, they can drain the people involved and leave them tired out. Often events that ought to be classified as 'pre-evangelism' (because the gospel is never shared with them) are thought of as 'evangelism'. The activities are put on with the best will in the world, i.e. to get people saved. However, because the gospel, "the power of God for salvation" (Rom 1:16), is not in this activity, no-one is getting saved! So this leads to disappointment and even frustration. For this church, something must be done in the evangelism column—and fast.

In the church with the second diagram, the 'saints' are getting well fed—engorged, in fact—but what about 'the sinners'? This profile suggests that this much-edified church has lost sight of the Mission and, rather than taking the gospel to the nations (like Matt 28:18-20 mentions), it has become introverted. This is not just a problem for the non-Christian world not being reached by this congregation, but it is a problem for the church itself. Without the overarching goal of mission, churches tend to implode; they collapse in on themselves. If the energy is not spent getting the gospel out to the lost world, it is spent getting the specks of dust out of our brother's eye, or some other equally worthy activity! The Corinthian church had plenty of problems, and, from the way Paul writes to them, it seems that their problems arose from forgetting that there was gospel work to do. For this second church, something must be done in the evangelism column—and fast.

The same problem, looked at in another way, would arise if some goals lacked any boxes in their columns. For example, this church:

	EVANGELISM				EDIFICATION		
ACTIVITY	Raising Awareness	Initial Contact	Pre-Evangelism	Evangelism	Follow-up	Nurture	Training in Ministry
Ladies Coffee morning			■	□			
Simply Christianity Course				■			
Doorknock Evangelism Explosion		■		■			■
Trained Nurturer's					■		
Bible study						■	

This church needs to decide whether they wish to 'raise awareness' more in their community, perhaps through a catchy ad in the local paper, or a 'sandwich board' on the nearby busy highway, or a letter box drop, or whatever.

Or this church:

	EVANGELISM				EDIFICATION		
ACTIVITY	Raising Awareness	Initial Contact	Pre-Evangelism	Evangelism	Follow-up	Nurture	Training in Ministry
Church				■		■	
Guest Services				■			
Evangelism Explosion				■			■
Newspaper ad	■						
Coffee morning			■	□			
Sign on highway	■						

They obviously have a lot of evangelistic activities set up, but with nothing aiming at 'initial contact' they may find that eventually they have no-one to evangelize any more. This may lead to some plans to begin to rub shoulders with a new bunch of non-Christians: a doorknock perhaps; or a strategy to visit some institution like a prison, or a hospital, or an office block, or a place of education; a questionnaire at the railway station in the afternoon rush; a plan to encourage congregation members to join a sporting club, or to hold a street Christmas party, or a post-election BBQ.

If there are columns with nothing in them, it doesn't necessarily mean that something *must* be put into that column immediately. Sometimes it *does* mean this. For example, if there is no direct evangelism going on, or any edification of the believers, something is seriously amiss and the situation needs to be rectified *now.* But some activities may not be as crucial. A church may be doing nothing specifically to 'raise awareness', but may still have a flood of people turning up to the church, being evangelized and so on. It might be perfectly appropriate to leave that column blank for the time being. Later, when the flood of people may drop off, it may be time to re-assess whether some specific activity should be targeted to raise awareness once again. However, a blank column certainly means that the situation needs to be assessed. If it is left blank, it should be done so after some hard thinking, and after a commitment to re-assess this decision when circumstances change.

We have now strayed beyond simple analysis, which is where we began. But that is not a bad thing, for it is the step that follows naturally. So why don't we turn to this next use of the tool: Planning.

Chapter 4

Planning towards mission

Once you have analysed your occasionally/usually/constantly/eternally (strike out whatever is inapplicable) maintenance-oriented church, if you still have the energy you no doubt want to ask a very simple question: 'What next?'.

I'm glad you asked. 'What next' is to do some planning that will take you closer towards mission. This may be done by the pastor; it may be done by a committee; it may be done by both pastor and committee, and perhaps even more people than that! But the important thing is that it is done!

► *Plugging the Dangerous Holes.* As mentioned in the last chapter, the analysis may have revealed certain imbalances in the church's activities. Let's say, for example, that there was a whole host of things in the Pre-Evangelism column, and absolutely nothing in the Evangelism column. This could easily happen, because it is easy to confuse the two. You see, Christians have a heart for getting people converted and so they have an evangelistic *desire.* This desire can result in all kinds of activities which are set up in great hope that they will get people converted. But the fact is that often there is *no specific plan to verbally share the gospel, and it is this verbal sharing of the gospel that is evangelism.* No matter how much evangelistic desire we have, unless the gospel is shared, the activity is Pre-Evangelism not Evangelism. But when there is a lot of evangelistic desire there are bound to be a lot of activities that have sprung out of that desire, and so, almost without noticing it, a church can generate many items which ought to be properly labelled Pre-Evangelism, sometimes to the neglect of Evangelism itself.

Sometimes this blockage can even be caused by our misguided thinking about evangelism. There are some approaches that stress the need for 'building relationships', or for 'building bridges to the community', or for 'earning the right to evangelize', and such like. The truth in this statement is that you have to have contact with people before you can talk to them about Jesus. But the problem is that we can spend so much time building the bridge, that we never get around to crossing it! (Is it the right time? Is the bridge built strong enough? Have I built up enough 'credibility'? etc). Such thinking also gives us a good justification for the natural fear we all have about telling our friends about Jesus. I might be afraid to do so, but now I can just say that it is not the appropriate time! If we are thinking like this about Evangelism, the likelihood is that we will have multiplied pre-evangelistic activities.

	EVANGELISM				EDIFICATION		
ACTIVITY	Raising Awareness	Initial Contact	Pre-Evangelism	Evangelism	Follow-up	Nurture	Training in Ministry
Coffee morning			■				
Men's mechanics night			■				
Men's golf day			■				
Bush dance			■				
Carols by Candlelight			■				

This church needs to recognise that this situation is not good (for nobody will get converted if the gospel is not shared—that is just a fact of life), and then decide what can be done to rectify the situation. Through reflection on the Bible, they realise that the solution consists of proclaiming the gospel, for it is *the gospel* that is the power of God for salvation to everyone who believes—not the young mums' playgroup, no matter how excellently it is run! So the planners must take this into account and plan something that will give this church an evangelistic edge.

► *Deciding NOT to plug some holes.* However, although there must always be something in the Evangelism column, there may be certain other deficits that are deemed acceptable, given the stage of life the church is at. For instance, the 'Raising Awareness' column may be very thin. Its only representative may be that the church building has a sign out front and is located on a reasonably major road. Other activities may be canvassed to fill this lack (advertising in the local paper, a letterbox drop, beer coasters in the local club with the service times on them, a banner behind a plane on Grand Final Day!), but all of them require more money than you have to spend. As well as this, there are heaps of people already in contact with the church through the multitude of Pre-Evangelistic activities, so the need to raise awareness is not so urgent at this stage. The decision can be legitimately made not to do anything about this lack now, but it will be reviewed when circumstances change.

► *Pruning Activities.* On the other hand, the analysis may actually force you to consider whether there are too many activities in the Pre-Evangelism column. Perhaps these activities are demanding lots of time and energy, and maybe also money. Perhaps you have noticed that it is fairly hard to maintain the motivation of the Christians who are involved, for they seem to put in so much but see so little fruit for their effort: "Nobody seems to be getting converted and we've been at it for so long now". Perhaps it is time to prune some of these Pre-Evangelistic activities (which will never get anyone converted without some specific evangelism) and institute some specific Evangelism. Once this decision is made, what happens then?

Target Groups

Here is another use for the tool. Whenever an activity is listed in the left-hand column, it is very helpful to also list its 'Target Group' as clearly as possible. For instance, a playgroup is by its very nature aimed at non-working mothers with pre-school children. (If in doubt about who the target group actually is, go along to the activity and ask yourself, what do all these people have in common? That question will begin to provide some answers.)

► *Think before you prune.* However, you may notice that your church has three playgroups running. A trap for the young player would be to decide immediately to axe two of the groups, in the interests of cleaning out the Pre-Evangelism column. After all, they all have the same label ('Playgroup'), and it seems inefficient to have three, and oh-so-neat to have only one group assigned to each label. But this would definitely be a trap, and the young player must beware of falling into it. The fact is that a church might have several playgroups running on different days or at different times which are suitable for different people. They may draw mothers from different geographical locations, since neighbours tend to bring neighbours along. They might draw mothers from different sociological groups, since the single mum on a pension can't afford to keep up with the dress standards of the 'twin-set and pearls' group of mums that attend playgroup after their tennis morning. So, even though you may have three 'Playgroups' listed in your left-hand column, when target groups are analysed more closely you end up with:

Playgroup: Non-working on Tuesday Morning mothers from area A.
Playgroup: Non-working on Thursday Morning mothers from area B.
Playgroup: Non-working on Friday Morning mothers from area A & B.

A check of the attendance rolls also confirms that there are three distinct groups of women coming along. Conclusion: these are three distinct activities under the aim of Pre-Evangelism. If there is no other good reason to stop one or more of these, then it would be a mistake to wield the razor just because the Pre-Evangelism column looked too full. They all seem to be performing a useful function, and they are not overlapping at all.

However, the target group analysis may reveal that this is not the case with some other activities. You may find that the craft group, the women's guild, the Friday coffee morning and the monthly women's Saturday get together all have as their target group women in the 40-50 year age bracket. A check on rolls also reveals that the ten or twelve ladies in that bracket attend all of these groups. Not only that, but each group is run by a different person in the church, so there seems to be an obvious waste of human resources upon this small group of ladies. Conclusion: a decision needs to be made about whether some pruning needs to occur within *this particular set* of Pre-Evangelistic activities.

► *Church Planning according to Target Group.* Target groups are an excellent way to structure the planning of a church's activities, even beyond the help it provides in analysis. In the left-hand column, activities can be grouped according to their target. Churches usually have age-related groups, and often sex-type related groups, which could give a left-hand column as follows:

Pre-schoolers Creche (9am Sunday) Playgroup							
School-age (Primary) Tuesday Kids Club Sunday School							
Secondary School Friday Fellowship							
Adult (Men) Men's BBQ quarterly							
Adult (Women) Women's Bible Study							

Listing out the functions performed by each group can then enable the planning of where and how each person in that age group is being evangelized, edified or trained in ministry.

► *Planning according to the Mission fields.* But it can go further than just the groups traditionally run by churches (we don't want to wallow in 'Maintenance Mode' any longer, do we?!). Now we are on the way to Mission, we want to think beyond the activities we already have. Jesus urged his followers to "lift up their eyes and see the fields are ripe for harvest" (Jn 4:35; see also Matt 9:37). It is not that the harvest is not there; it is just that we don't lift up our eyes and see it. There are harvest fields all around us. Every single member of your congregation is standing in their own unique harvest-field. They just have to see it. The rest of us just have to help each other to see all the many harvest fields that are around.

The tool can help us to do this. If the left-hand column is given to the target groups we wish to reach, then the remainder of the columns can be filled in as we plan how each group is to be contacted, evangelized, edified, etc.

Another example: suppose your suburb has had a big influx of a certain racial group which you feel needs to be reached for the gospel (a perfectly right feeling!). List this group in the left-hand column, then go across the other goals and plan how you will raise awareness, contact and evangelize *this particular group*. Or suppose you notice there are no teenagers in your church, and yet everywhere you look in the suburb they are crawling up the lamp-posts and sliding around street corners, and you decide they are a group that needs to be reached. What do you do? Put them in the left-hand column and then plan each step through the other columns. Your page may end up something like this:

South Africans								
Filipinos								
Teenagers								
Elderly								
Unemployed								
Single mums								
Business people								

Once such planning is done, you should have a fairly comprehensive diagram across your piece of paper—your 'Mission Minded' tool. At a glance in the left-hand column you can see the activity and the target group. Reading across the columns you can see what activities perform what functions, now hopefully in dark boxes rather than dotted ones. (Although some will always have a blurred or multiple function, most should have a clearly defined aim—it helps to know what you are trying to hit!) This will be an extremely useful document. Guard it with your life!

Such a document will enable the groups to know clearly who they are trying to reach, and what they are trying to achieve with these people. That will help them do it. It will also enable the right people to be invited to the right activity. And that is the heart of ministry, isn't it? For isn't ministry about a particular kind of service to a particular kind of person with a specific kind of need? That is what we ought to turn to right now. But it can wait until chapter 5, if you insist.

Chapter 5

Mission means people

Ministry is really quite simple, even though, as with anything, we simple people have a tendency to make the simple things too complex to handle. But ministry is simple, at least in its basics. For isn't ministry about three P's? It is about **Proclamation** —telling people about Jesus, preaching the gospel, evangelizing people. It is about **Prayer**—asking God to work through his Word, like he promises to do. It is about **People**—loving them, caring enough about them to speak the truth of God's word to them, whether it is convenient or inconvenient for them. **P**roclaiming, **P**raying, **P**eople-ing: that is Christian ministry.

Now, the trouble with being susceptible to Maintenance Mode, is that we too easily get stuck in the rut of simply maintaining 'structures'. That is, we run groups and activities and programs and meetings and more meetings. Now, all of that sounds very different to the three P's, doesn't it? And let me assure you, all of that is nowhere near as exciting as being involved in real Christian ministry! And let me tell you another thing, the reason it is not nearly so exciting is that God doesn't promise to work through 'meetings'—and he very rarely does! God promises to work through his Word (proclamation), in response to our requests (prayers) for John, Mary, Minh Tan, Xerxes and Abdul (people)—

and he actually does! And that is what makes Christian ministry exciting.

It doesn't help us either when so much of the world's understanding of Christianity is far from the real thing. Many people —both church people and non-church people—define Christianity *organizationally* ('What's the official line on…') or *formally* (as if it is only about church services on Sunday). It is very easy for pastors to begin to see themselves merely as people who function in a certain role that is prescribed by the community around them, or the expectations of the people in their local congregation or, worse still, their distant denomination. They begin to 'do a job', like any other person, except it is 'The Ministry'. They can even be heard to talk as if they had a career path within their organization (read 'denomination'), and some have even talked of 'job satisfaction'. Yuk! But all of that is the maintenance rut that is so easy to slip into. Ministry is service of Christ in his mission to a lost world. And this kind of ministry—real ministry—is simply proclamation, prayer and people.

So far we have applied the tool to analysing and planning the structures of a church. I began at this end because, if we really are in the maintenance rut, that is exactly what we think ministry is! If we are wallowing down there—either permanently or just momentarily—we will envisage ministry in terms of what activities and groups and programs our church is involved in. Well, the tool is a help for all these things, and they all do have their place, and so we have begun with these things.

However, if ministry is about people, we have to move on to another way of thinking and another use of the tool, perhaps an even more important use. Another cliché of the Mission Mafia is that ministry is 'people not programs'—keep that one under your belt for when they next turn up! (If you drop it in conversation it earns at least 10 extra points on the 'Good Guy' list.) Programs do have their place, but they must never be allowed to eclipse the fact that we care about people: people who are lost *without* Christ; people who are found for eternity *with* Christ. That is why we must move on to a further use of this tool.

But let's get there slowly. Why rush things? Let's rejoin our newly arrived pastor. He has analysed the structures of the church, and done some planning, so that he now knows what the church structures are aiming to do and who they are aiming to do it to. Now, how does he 'get people involved'?

'Getting people involved'

A common method is the smorgasbord approach. Don't get me wrong, I like the smorgasbord approach—but in restaurants, not in churches. In the right place, it is great to be offered everything and have the freedom to eat what you like, when you like—which usually means everything, and all night! But in churches this doesn't seem to be the way to go. What usually happens is that we offer everyone everything and they end up with indigestion as a result.

For example, if we do a leaflet drop, why list every conceivable activity that the church has going and tell them that they are welcome to anything and everything they like? If someone gets converted and is really keen, why make sure that they are involved in everything that is going? Is it because we have to nab them while their initial keenness lasts? If there is a church activity, why is it an unwritten eleventh commandment that the whole church must be involved? Is it because we feel it is a threat to unity if every single member doesn't turn up?

► *Principled Invitations.* But our newly arrived pastor knows better. Now that he clearly knows what each activity is trying to achieve, he will invite people to be involved in *only what is relevant for them.* Are they non-Christian? He looks down his Evangelism column and invites them to the 'Simply Christianity' course. Are they Christian but needing to know the basics? He looks down his Edification columns before hitting them with the idea of some personal follow-up, spilling into one of the Bible Study groups. Are they involved in a pre-evangelistic activity? Well, he would never even think of inviting them to another such activity; he will ask them to something evangelistic next.

► *Invite to the Right.* There are a number of principles which operate once the activities of a church are itemized and analysed. Remember that the movement is towards the right. Therefore, that is the direction of invitations as well. If someone is already contacted, he doesn't need to be made aware. If they are converted, they don't need to be evangelized for the first time! The invitation ought to be towards the right, not the left. That is one principle.

► *Invite to one similar thing at a time.* Another is like it, namely, that the invitations ought to be towards the right. Sound the same? Yes it is, only this time I mean that the invitations ought to be towards the right, *not up or down the column at the one time.* Let me explain. It seems that people like to concentrate on one thing. If someone is asked to do too many things it doesn't allow them to concentrate on the one thing that is essential at that time. For example, if someone is going to a playgroup (= Pre-Evangelism), it doesn't make sense to ask them to a coffee morning with the same pre-evangelistic aim. It uses up their time a little more, and so competes with a more worthwhile activity that you may be able to invite them to. Let me say it again: no-one gets converted through pre-evangelism; they need to hear the gospel. No matter how many pre-evangelisms they are into, they still won't get converted. If they are in the playgroup then *no ground is made at all* if they are also invited to the coffee morning—in fact, ground may well be lost. What they need to be invited to is not something up or down the same column, but something in the *next column to the right.* They need to be moved out of Pre-Evangelism into Evangelism.

There may come a time when they tire of one kind of pre-evangelism or outgrow it—for instance, their preschooler goes to school and they therefore cannot come to playgroup. Then, if such an activity is still thought necessary, it may be the time to invite her to the coffee morning. But it will be better still to get her out of pre-evangelism altogether and into something that will give her the gospel and help her to get converted. However, if pre-evangelism is all that she seems to want at this stage, then a (reluctant) invitation up or down the Pre-Evangelism column can be made. In doing so, however, we ought to realise that even though she may seem 'more involved' (because this will now be the second activity she has used), in terms of our mission goals, *absolutely no ground has been made.* Pre-evangelism remains pre-evangelism and nothing more. And, in case you have missed it so far I will say it again—it won't get anyone converted by itself.

► *Never move backwards.* There is a third principle. Just as invitations should be towards the right, and invitations ought not to be up or down the same column at the same time, so also it is a firm rule that *you never move backwards.* This may be rule one in disguise, but it is important enough to say it anyway! (Let's call it a corollary of the rule about moving to the right.) If Mr Normal—'Norm' for short—has just had a child and, for whatever reason felt only to him (and it *will* be felt, hardly ever *thought*), he approaches his local baby-baptizing institution, which happens to be your church, what do you do with him? Do you send him away so you can Raise his Awareness first? No, he is not only aware of where the church is, but also that it provides a baptism service, and even that this is vaguely to do with 'God'. Do you try to establish Initial Contact with Norm, perhaps asking for his address so that the doorknock team can call on him to explain where your church is and that he would be welcome to come anytime? No! Don't be stupid. He's standing there on your doorstep: contact has been made—from his side, at least! Do you ask him along to a Pre-Evangelism activity so he can 'build relationships' with some of the people at church? No, you don't even need to do this. In fact, you *must not* do this—it is an invitation that moves him backwards. Norm hasn't arrived to 'build relationships'; he has arrived for the baptism of his child. In the present day situation, this usually means that he has kindly presented you with an opportunity for Evangelism. Now, if Norm is standing there asking to be evangelized, it is ridiculous to shove him into something that won't give him the gospel in a direct, forthright and clear way, asking him for a decision en route. Once Norm arrives on the doorstep there is only one kind of invitation he needs and that is the invitation of the gospel. You *never move backwards*.

Even if he doesn't respond to the first gospelling activity—in this case, the baptismal interviews in which it is your policy to share the gospel at least three times—and you want to know what to do next, you still don't move him backwards. Now is the time to bounce him up and down in the same column. He needs to be given as many opportunities to be evangelized as you've got going, one after the other, and then you have to invent some more! Never lose ground, always move ahead.

What if his interest seems to wane and nothing has happened? Well, some people may think a bit of Pre-Evangelism could be good for him—a couple of games of golf with the church men, an invitation to bring his family to the church bush dance or BBQ—and certainly this may be of some use. But (and here is what this principle is trying to drive home), once he has entered your scheme of things at the level of 'Please Evangelize Me', then you have to keep evangelizing him—that is the only polite thing to do! If he seems to cool off, perhaps the strategy should be to keep just the right amount of evangelistic pressure on him at the level he has reached so far. If he has done

Simply Christianity and decided not to go on to your next evangelistic activity, you can still keep before him the challenge that *Simply Christianity* left him with: the occasional phone call, centering upon the decision that he knows he has to make; the occasional reminder to him about the urgency of deciding for Jesus. During this time, you may decrease the frequency with which you are inviting him to evangelistic *activities* but you should still maintain contact with him as *a person who needs, and now knows he needs, to make a decision for Christ*. And, of course, he knows that you will contact him when there is an important evangelistic activity on as well, for by now he knows that you want him to have as many opportunities as possible! But our point is clear: you *never move backwards*. Whatever your strategy with Norm, don't lose ground—always aim at evangelism.

As for the Christians of your congregation, this aspect of the tool helps with them too, but this can wait until chapter 7.

YWMMWY

► *Opportunities for training*. There is one exception to these absolutely unbreakable rules! The one time when it is legitimate to give an invitation 'to the left' is when you wish to involve someone in an activity for the sake of their ministry. A keen Christian man may be invited to join an 'Investigating Christianity' group with five non-Christian men. Why? Not because he needs to be evangelized—for goodness sake, he is so thoroughly converted that the angels in heaven have long ago stopped their celebrations—but because you want him to learn how to evangelize others. He is in the group to watch you do it, so that he can then do it too, on his own eventually. (He will do a much better job after he watches you if you then watch him and give feedback for his further training. This is the YWMMWY method of training in ministry: You Watch Me, Me Watch You.) Someone may well get an invitation to the left, even though it is for another reason. It needs to be *for their sake*. And so it ends up being an invitation to the right, for it is an invitation to the column headed 'Training In Ministry'.

Watch this one. In Maintenance Mode these kind of invitations to 'Be Involved With X or Y' are often issued, mostly at the end of the year or at the beginning of a new one. They usually operate on the 'vacuum principle', that is, a hole is opened up so quickly that someone is sucked into it in the rush! They go like this: at announcement time in the church meeting someone stands up with a real worried look on his face and says, "There's a desperate need for more teachers in the Sunday School. You should all feel guilty if you don't meet this urgent need. The children of today are the church of tomorrow." He sits down and everyone *does* feel guilty. But no-one responds except for that young girl who can't say no to anything and is already running fourteen classes from the previous invitations! Notice how this kind of invitation works: we have a need in Structure X; therefore fill it up! People are dangled over a hole in a messy structure which needs patching.

► *People sent to serve.* This is not the way forward at all. Nobody ought to be doing a job—oops… that is not the way to say it. Nobody ought to have a ministry to a group of people unless they are gifted for that ministry and unless they themselves will benefit from being involved in it. Their sphere of service ought to be a help to their own Christian development—they should be getting trained as they serve. This doesn't mean that they aren't asked to do a thing until they decide they have the gifts or desire the training; that is not their privilege. It is their church's privilege and responsibility to open up ministries for them. People are called to be Christians (by God in his gospel), but they are sent into ministries (by their fellow believers who recognise their gifts). This means that the church ought to think long and hard about each person before inviting anyone to exercise a ministry anywhere.

Do you see the direction we are approaching things from? We don't move from the structure (with a gaping hole in it) to the people (who are now merely gap-fillers), but we move *from the people to the ministry* to which they are peculiarly suited in the opinion of their church. You see, if mission is about people, and ministry is about people, then the converse is true as well: people are about ministry. But this is our next chapter. Let's leave it until then.

Chapter 6

People mean ministry

Now that we are re-oriented to think about ministry from the people end, the beauty of the tool becomes even more apparent. For it enables us to plan out a strategy for our ministry to each and every individual within our care.

► *Your ministry to non-Christians.* Take out your piece of paper and put the goals along the top once again. Above the left-hand column, write: 'Non-Christian contacts'. Then list out all the non-Christian people that you are seeking to bring to Christ—without whom they are lost; with whom they are gloriously saved. (This should be simply a re-listing of your prayer list—but I won't put it that way lest I make you feel guilty about lapsing into Maintenance Mode in your prayers as well.)

Now go across the columns and **analyse** what ministry each has received. How was their awareness raised? Do you know? If so, write it in. If not, why not ask them next time you visit them? How was initial contact made? Write it in. And was there a pre-evangelism bit to their story? Write it in. What opportunities to hear the gospel have you given them? List these out in the Evangelism column.

Having analysed your ministry to the first person on your list: what will be your next step? You learn fast, of course: **planning**.

What evangelistic opportunity are you going to take with them next? Will you invite them to a short series of evangelistic Bible studies? Will you invite them to the guest service coming up next August? Will you go around and ask them the two 'Evangelism Explosion' questions (no doubt I should put a copyright symbol on these somewhere—make sure you do if you use them!)? Will you give them an evangelistic book or tape or video or...? Whatever it is, write in your plan, then grab your diary and arrange a time to do it.

	EVANGELISM			
Non-Christian Contacts	Raising Awareness	Initial Contact	Pre-Evangelism	Evangelism
Ima Nunbeliever	Newspaper advert	Phone call to me	–	Shared "2 Ways to Live" 6/2/99. Simply Christianity April-June 99 Guest service – July 99 Video given – August 99 **Plan:** – Invite to "Investigating Christianity" beginning Feb 2000 – personal conversation: try to find out why he has not made a decision so far – ring and arrange **tonight**

It is now time to move onto the next person on your prayer list. What have you done? What will you do next? When will you do it?

► *Your ministry to Christians.* Once you have gone through your non-Christian prayer list, have a breather, then get out your Christian prayer list or your church roll or your Bible Study group roll or your 'these are the people I have a ministry to' roll. Take out the now familiar rectangular piece of paper with the columns and put at the top of the left-hand side 'Church' (or something equally descriptive). Then put down number one: 'Alexander Aardvark'. What ministry have you exercised with his benefit in mind? Or what ministry is being exercised towards him and by whom (for it needn't, and eventually cannot, always be you)? Write it all down. Okay, now the planning: what (further) ministry does Big Al need? Or, what (further) ministry does the one already having a ministry to Big Al need? Write it down, then get your diary and you know what comes next. Then do person number two. And so on.

► *Assisting your 'TIMs'.* The tool is also helpful in deciding what kind of ministry a person ought to be trained in. Grab another piece of rectangular Mission Goals paper and give the left-hand column the heading 'Training in Ministry'. List out your key people (that is, anyone who is not an extremely new Christian, for every Christian will have a ministry of some kind—notice that even the blind man in John 9 and the cured Gerasene demoniac in Mark 5 weren't given too long to cool their heels before being sent off into the harvest field). Now begin to think about training them in ministry. How will you do it?

Whatever you do must be helpful to them and a fitting avenue for their gifts to be used. Use the tool to think about them.

- *Raising Awareness:* Is Mr Aardvark someone who could write the copy for a weekly newspaper advertisement? Is he retired with plenty of energy, enough for a daily walk during which he could drop leaflets in letterboxes? Has the doctor ordered him to take a daily walk following his triple by-pass—an even stronger indication of his spiritual giftedness in this area?!
- *Initial Contact:* Is he a friendly, outgoing sort of guy who has the ability to make people feel relaxed and comfortable? Would he be suitable for the doorknock team, or the 'Welcomers' at church on Sunday morning?
- *Evangelism:* Does he know the gospel? Is he keen to save the lost? Can he explain the gospel? Has he been already doing this?
- *Edification:* Does he know his Bible well? Is he an able teacher? Is he reliable?

And so on. Then turn to your diary and arrange a time at which you can get together with AA, talk over his giftedness, and thrust him into the ministry he is suited for. At the same time you can outline the training opportunities that he will be given and how he will receive the ongoing encouragement that every Christian should receive as they are involved in ministry. Now for the next person on your list.

The tool can also help to think through with someone their giftedness for a particular ministry. Although some people may find it hard to say where their strengths lie, working through the tool with them may help to clarify or open up a sphere of service for them. On the other hand, some people may have the unfortunate situation of being TOO gifted, and a discussion over the tool may help them to concentrate where they are most needed, or where they will be of most strategic benefit. We should also remember that people and ministries can change over time. It also seems like a person's ministry is to some extent determined by their own stage in the Christian life.

So, for example, a new convert is keen about the gospel. She is keen to 'get involved'. Raising awareness seems easy, because she certainly has the energy to put leaflets in the letter boxes. But she is really uncomfortable about knocking on doors—not because she is not keen, just because she doesn't think she knows enough. You organize with her to teach her a gospel outline and to answer some questions. With a month or two of input, she is keen about the doorknock. Who knows where she will go next?

Or again, the church has grown and there are many people wanting to get into Bible study groups. But who will teach them? Bob has been around for a while, but doesn't think he can do the group leading thing. But he can sit in with another leader for a while, even with the fancy title 'co-leader', and take the odd lead when he is able, under the watchful eye of his leader. Eventually, he has his own group and his nurturing ministry is well-received.

Bob's wife, Mary, just goes to water when she thinks of speaking in public. But when she is with one or two, you can't stop her! She remembers fondly how someone helped her when she first became a Christian. Would she like to be involved in follow-up? There is a young girl just converted, how about meeting with her? Two months down the track, two friends of this girl are converted, and the one-to-one is forced to become one-to-three! Mary is rejoicing that her ministry is now to a group—and it hasn't been too painful at all!

Once all this hard work is over, it becomes obvious that such thinking enables you to care more effectively for the most valuable resource your church has got: its people. Once a person's Training in Ministry opportunity is decided (with their consultation and agreement, of course), then it will prevent everyone from being over-committed, mobilize more people into ministry, prevent burn out, and even stop the gap-filling approach, because the gaps will be filled before they even open up!

► *Ministry is to individuals.* I know what you are saying: "Where am I going to get the time to do all this? It is far easier to just keep the group going as it is." That is true. Maintenance is easier than mission. But it is also far less effective for reaching the world for Christ. Paul wrote: "We proclaim him, admonishing and teaching everyone with all wisdom, so that we may present everyone perfect in Christ. To this end I labour, struggling with all his energy, which so powerfully works in me" (Col 1:28-29). His ministry was directed towards 'everyone', that is, each person at an individual, personal level. It involved all the God-given energy that he had. And he used it because the goal of maturity/perfection for all was so important in the plan of God. Surely this should be our pattern of ministry as well. Isn't ministry about encouraging each person onwards towards maturity in Christ? If we feel we have too little time to plan out a ministry strategy for each individual, perhaps that indicates it is time to share the load. Is this why Paul had his team around him—Timothy and the rest? Is it time to more actively involve other elders in the church in such caring for people? Is it time we put on another pastor? Enlisted more helpers for the ministry? Prayed for more labourers to be sent out into the harvest field?

Mission means people. People mean ministry. Our tool can help us focus upon our mission (which is Christ's mission), and provide ministry to our people (who are Christ's people). And it is not just helpful to a pastor of a church—anyone involved in ministry to any group of people can get out that sheet of paper and work out a strategy for their ministry to the members of their youth group or Bible Study or the people at work or school or whatever. Mission means people; people mean ministry.

But one more thing remains. Ministry needs to be supported in various ways, and the tool can help here as well. It is to this new and different category of 'Support to Ministry' that we now turn.

Chapter 7

Supporting Christian ministry

I know I'm doing something naughty by making a distinction between 'Ministry' (i.e. something that directly serves the gospelling or edification of people) and 'Support to Ministry'. However, I feel that it is a useful distinction, for it enables us to keep the focus on our mission goals and see how other things serve these goals. It is all too easy for things in this supportive category to gain an importance that they don't warrant.

Take, for instance, a working bee. Sure, it does *indirectly* serve the work of the kingdom, but it only does so *indirectly*. If we hold a working bee every day of the week until Christ returns, nobody will be converted, and nobody will necessarily progress towards maturity. It does not contribute *directly* to the work of ministry, although no doubt it would contribute directly to the work of blisters. Or take committee work and its office bearers, who are often given the status that goes with personalized nametags printed with their title underneath in oversized capitals. Sure, they do a job that is necessary and important, and, biblically speaking, it is a ministry—probably the gift of "helps and administrations" (1 Cor 12:28). But if all the Christian church did was run committee meetings, the kingdom of God would not advance very far. And unfortunately there is a lot of evidence in many churches and across denominations to back up that claim! To separate 'Support to Ministry' into its own category enables such roles and meetings to function with a clear idea of what they are doing: *they are never an end in themselves, but they support the real work of the gospel.*

► *Rosters.* The same goes for the various rosters; morning tea, washing up, gardening, cleaning, etc. These are all supportive ministries in that they support the ministry of the gospel. It is all too easy for people to be on every cleaning roster and at every working bee and be elected to wear every nametag that's going, and then have no time or inclination or feel any compulsion to be involved in the real work. If we let people see that such things are ministries in the same category as Evangelism and Edification, then the excuse 'I did my bit for the church—the working bee takes three hours of my time each month' becomes perfectly valid. In this busy world that is a lot of time! Every year, most churches have an Annual General Meeting which forces us to elect office bearers to Support the Ministry. The danger is that this annual pressure might put good people into supportive roles, when they should be in ministry roles. Time often says that they can't do both, and so we may have the ludicrous situation in which the talents of people who should be leading Bible studies or preaching the gospel or training others in ministry have been hijacked, leaving them to fall asleep at the monthly committee meeting. The mission goals should help us to maintain priorities: encourage those gifted people to get into ministry, and let others take care of supporting the ministry. The danger is that so many people can be used up *supporting* the ministry that no-one is *doing* the (much harder but far more rewarding) ministry that will actually win the lost and edify and equip the saints.

► *Prayer Meeting.* There are other things that can be called a Support to Ministry—the weekly prayer meeting, for example. Please don't get nervous at this point. To say that the function of Prayer is 'support to ministry' is not to denigrate prayer in any way. We have already noticed how important prayer is, because isn't ministry Proclamation, Prayer and People? Prayer has a vital role, and all of our activities and ministries ought to be conducted with prayer. But, that illustrates the function: prayer is a vitally important *support to ministry.*

But so often prayer meetings can degenerate into asking God to heal Aunt Mildred's sore toenail. (What, is that *still* a problem? It must be—no matter where you pray or when you pray it seems to always come up!) Now, of course God likes dealing with ingrown toenails as much as the rest of us, and it ought to be prayed for by someone, somewhere. But at the church prayer meeting? Every week? By so many people? By making it known that the prayer meeting is a Support to Ministry, the prayers are immediately focused on the mission **goals** that this church is working towards, on the **people** targeted to be reached, on the **edification** of the congregation, on **those being trained** for ministry. Now *there* is a prayer meeting! And because the goals are drawn from the Bible, we know that we are praying according to God's will. And let me tell you, that prayer meeting will be an exciting thing to be a part of as God does what he promises and answers prayers time and again!

► *Giving.* Then there is giving. Yes, I am talking about money. Why do we pass the plate around at everything bar the morning tea (you *do*???)? Isn't it to support the mission of this church? Isn't it to provide resources that are needed to further the goals that we have? Isn't it to support the ministry of the gospel? This focuses our giving, for without this financial support perhaps the goals will not be reached as effectively. Giving can't be an end in itself. The person who does his bit for the church by tossing his twenty cents in the plate may be supporting the ministry (fairly minimally, no doubt), but he is still not being trained in the ministry or being part of it yet. (What goal do you have for him on your piece of paper?) He is merely *supporting* the ministry, not *doing* it.

► *Reviewing, Monitoring and Financing.* Having justified the distinction a little, I also need to add that this tool can help us with these Supports to Ministry. We have already seen how the Mission goals can focus a prayer meeting, and how they can help a pastor or committee analyse and plan. But committees have other functions as well. After planning according to the Mission goals, they can then review and monitor progress throughout the year, and keep things going according to the goals they set for the various activities. They usually have some role in funding various activities, and the goals can shape the apportioning of funds. The treasurer can get out his piece of paper, put 'Money' at the top of the left-hand column and list out all the things that money is spent on in the budget. He can then go across the goals columns and fill in his dark boxes to see what goals are being funded by this church. Is the cash going into Ministry or is it going into Support for Ministry (buildings, grounds, etc.)? It is a good idea for budgets to be set after the planning of goals, so that the committee first asks *What should we do*? and only then asks *How shall we fund our goals?*, not *How much have we got?* then *What will we spend it on?*

► *Reviewing our People Resources.* When looking at our strategy for our ministry to people (our most valuable resource), this perhaps unbiblical distinction does come in handy. Are a lot of man-hours and cash and resources being spent on activities that are, in the end, only Support to Ministry? The danger is that if too many resources are being drained by Support to Ministry then there may not end up being any Ministry to support!

A related issue which can now be discussed (since we have now discussed the entire piece of paper) is the question of what and how much people ought to be involved in. It is easy to find people that are overburdened in the work of their church and, sadly, there are some whose overwork for the church helps them to forget the one they are meant to be serving. There are even people who burn out from too much church work, and end up burning out from Christian discipleship altogether. It is just as easy to think of people who don't contribute anything much to Christ's mission, but who have the view that they take what they please and have no obligation to give anything back.

We have already seen that the tool can aid our ministry to people. (In itself, the tool is therefore a support to ministry!) As we think about the people in our congregation we can put their names in the left-hand column and then map out the things they are involved in.

	EVANGELISM				EDIFICATION			SUPPORT TO MINISTRY
People	Raising Awareness	Initial Contact	Pre-Evangelism	Evangelism	Follow-up	Nurture	Training in Ministry	
John Smith	• Writes newspaper ad weekly	• Door-knock team	• Runs Men's mechanics night	• Monthly dialogue meeting • Hosts Simply Christianity		• Sunday church (2 services) • Thurs Bible study • Tues Bible Study • Correspondence course	• Writes newspaper ad weekly • Runs Youth Group	• Working bee • Committee (secretary) • Giving • Prayer meeting
Sally Green	–	–	–	–	–	• Sunday church (fortnightly)	–	–

► *'Normal' Requirements?* Then it gets difficult. It seems obvious that John Smith is doing far too much (how does he fit in his job as corporate executive of the largest company in Australia, and his wife and seven children, and his sick parents who live with them, and…) and Sally Green has a fairly minimal involvement. But, what is the 'normal requirement' for a Christian engaged in Christ's Mission? What can be normally expected from each member of your congregation? It is a fact of life that people cannot be involved in all things going and expect to do all things well. It is also a fact of life that different people have different capacities and circumstances. But there may be some rule of thumb that can be worked out.

For a start, a person should be at the weekly congregational meeting (usually known as the 'Church Service') in which the Word of God is publicly proclaimed and prayers are said in response. This is a time when the Word of God sets the agenda for the work of the gospel in the week to come, a 'rallying point' for this group of Christians. Secondly, it is fairly usual nowadays to have a small group network in which the Word of God is discussed and applied and prayers are said in a more personal way than is possible in the weekly public meeting. The third expectation might be that every person is engaged in one thing for the purpose of ministry, since we should also be giving of ourselves to others, and whatever gifts we have been given are for the good of other people. Then, at the end of the list, there may also be a Support to Ministry activity that some people can also be involved in.

Once such 'Normal Expectations' are decided upon, at least as a rule of thumb, this enables you to talk with people about their 'load' and to suggest that they correct any deficiencies or drop any extra burdens that are spreading them too thin. In this process, of course, they will be moving into areas for which they are most gifted and out of those that others are more suited to.

Chapter 8

Back to the program

Back in Chapter 3, we talked about the structures that you might already find in place. Since then we have covered quite a lot of country, discovering on the way, amongst other things, that ministry is 'people not programs'. That may be a great relief to you. Every time it comes time to plan your program for the year or the month or even the day, you may go into a catatonic spasm for all I know, and so hearing this slogan is like hearing the good news of the gospel all over again! "No more programs!" I hear you yelling in delight, "No more planning! No more juggling dates! No more lining up events and speakers and... No more..."

Well, I'm sorry to break in upon this time of glee, but I have to. For the slogan 'People not Programs' is meant to focus our priorities; it is not meant to imply that there should be no programs at all. We do need a program, but it needs to have its proper place. It needs to serve the people. It needs to help them in their mission-oriented ministry.

Unfortunately, programs don't just happen—they need planning. The first step towards planning a program is to **plan when you will plan it**. At one end of the scale you have a daily routine, and at the other you have a yearly program. In between you have a weekly routine, and you may operate by month, or by school term. Whatever units of time you operate with, it is a good idea to set some time aside to plan your program for that time unit. And, of course, if you take the trouble to plan, it is also necessary to keep reviewing whether and how much you have achieved your plans, and so a regular time for **review** is also necessary.

But what enables such planning to be effective? Of course you know by now! The planning at the daily or weekly or monthly or term level will only be effective if the 'big picture' has also been worked out. That is, the logical order is to decide what our mission goals are—and our tool has provided that already—and then to plan an integrated overall program for the people in our church that aims to be as helpful to their mission as it can possibly be. This 'big picture' should generate the yearly program, and the yearly the monthly, and the monthly the weekly, and the weekly the daily. This means that, once the mission goals are adopted, a good period of time needs to be given to planning the year to come (and no doubt also reviewing the year that has just passed). Given the patterns in most churches, in Australia, at least, October seems to be a good time to do this. As for time needed, since it is so important, why not set aside a whole week to do it, perhaps planning to hold meetings with key groups and individuals to aid in this task?

But how do you plan an *integrated* and *mission helping* program? To do so, there seem to be three aspects of a church program that require thought. There are the regular 'maintenance' type structures, which, as we now understand, maintain people in their task of mission. There is the yearly program of events and activities, which, as we now understand, ought to help people in their task of mission. And there is the personal program of the pastor(s), which, as we will soon understand, ought to equip, facilitate and enthuse people for their task of mission.

1. Proper Maintenance

In Ephesians 4:15, Paul informs us that Christ's body (i.e. the congregation) grows as we speak the truth in love. Here he furnishes us with the key to proper maintenance: truth being spoken in love. This takes place at three levels: publicly, privately and individually.

Publicly

The truth ought to be spoken publicly at the regular congregational meetings/church services. Regular and systematic biblical preaching is essential to maintain the mission focus for a church. And, dare I say it, the preaching should be expository (that is, gradually seeking to explain the text of the Scriptures) rather than topical (that is, seeing what the Bible says on a topic of interest to us). Can you see why? If we are interested in being involved in *God's* mission, we need to allow him to set the agenda for us by dealing with the Bible in the way that he revealed it, rather than subtly setting our own agenda by always addressing the Bible with *our* questions and issues. Expository preaching allows the Word to address the world, and results in us seeing that world with God's eyes. Topical preaching allows the world to address the Word and results in us seeing both the world and the Word with our own eyes.

Having said that, there *is* a place for the topic—it can be used as exactly that: a topic. Once a preacher has understood the passage he will expound, he needs to ask himself: "How does this portion of God's Word address our world? What questions, desires, hopes, dreams, problems and pains does it address?" He can then use his answer to mould an appropriate topic for his expositional sermon. Remember my point: the members of the congregation need to be constantly reminded of the mission in which they are involved, and the goals which they are meant to pursue, and it is God's Word that will do this as it is regularly expounded in a systematic way. For then it is the Word which sets the agenda for both preacher and people.

Since the sermon is God's Word being addressed to a particular gathering of people, it ought to be the centre of whatever else occurs on Sunday (or whenever your church meets). Because God is at work in our midst, we should expect and plan for the fact that people will be present from all kinds of backgrounds—they may be converted or they may be still ignorant of God when they walk through the door that morning. Because the Word of God is addressed to any person present in the meeting, the whole meeting should be tailored so that no-one is hindered from hearing the Word of God. The Word of God for the day should issue in realistic prayer for the world and the congregation and their mission in the world. The songs should be selected as appropriate expressions of the joy that comes from hearing the Word of God yet again. In fact, the tone of everything that goes on should be filled with both the seriousness of listening to the living God, and the marvellous and deep joy that comes from hearing what he says. And then there is the love that needs to be present, not just love for those in the club, those so like ourselves, but the love of Christ for a lost world—the lost world that is there in our midst right at that very moment! The tragedy is that sometimes the things we do in church seem to ignore the fact that there is a world 'out there'.

Why say all this now? This vital part of the program also needs to be *planned*: what parts of the Bible will the preaching program include this year? What truth will be proclaimed publicly as part of the proper maintenance the congregation needs?

Privately

Then there is the proper maintenance that goes on privately. The basic unit, biblically speaking, is the family. In that setting, the truth of God ought to be spoken in love in the middle of all the ordinary pursuits of life (see Deut 6:4-9, Eph 6:4, 1 Cor 14:35). Certainly a church can plan ways to encourage and assist this kind of private teaching, and therefore make it part of the congregation's program. But it cannot be planned for in the same way as another private means of speaking the truth in love, that is, the small group network that exists within so many churches today.

Small groups perform functions that the public meeting cannot hope to do as adequately. They enable people to interact over God's Word, to ask questions, hear answers, to share applications, to pray together for more personal concerns, to learn to love whomever has been thrown together by the group, to begin to exercise gifts, to pray by name for the conversion of each other's non-Christian friends, to share the joy of seeing prayers answered, to receive personal attention and pastoral care from a small group of people and especially from the group leader, who really performs the role of pastor to that group. The fact is that when God causes a church to grow, it is this network of small groups that provides the context in which much of the pastoral care of a congregation goes on. One person cannot hope to care adequately for an entire congregation. With an adequate small group ministry, there is no need for one person to try!

An important step in planning, then, is to think about this very significant network where the Word of God is spoken in love privately. Are there adequate small groups to care for all the people in the congregation? If there are inadequate groups, then it will be hard to encourage everyone to join a group. The experts say that a good group number is about 8-12 people, so you can easily do the sums: in a congregation of 60 you need 5-7 groups; a congregation of 120 will need 10-15. Are there enough groups now? Will there be enough for the end of the year, after God 'adds to your numbers daily'? If not, your planning must include their increase.

And of course, that entails an increase in group leaders. This is often where the plot fails, for after all there is only one person in your entire congregation with nine and a half years of theological training, and you're already too busy! But don't be put off. Remember, firstly, that God causes gifts to emerge to meet needs—so pray! Then, secondly, remember that there are a variety of ways a group can be lead—a leader can do it all from his vast storehouse of wisdom and knowledge, or everyone can have a go with suitable direction from someone ready and able, or prepared material can be used, tapes can be listened to and discussed, videos can be watched, or a combination of many different things. And the good thing is that whoever leads or co-ordinates will be far better at it by the end of the year than they are now! So plan who your new leaders will be—if not this year, than certainly by next year, and then plan how you will use this year to get them ready. How will you train your new (and existing) leaders for their ministry. Plan a monthly leaders meeting. Plan the input you will give, and so on.

Then, of course, you need to plan how you are going to encourage people to join these groups. Public announcements? Public testimonies to their value? (When, how, how often?) Personal visits to encourage people to join particular groups? And so on.

Individually

The final place for speaking the truth in love is individually, one to one. Hopefully this will be a by-product of the public and private teaching of God's Word. But that is not all that can be done. Each member of the congregation needs to be stretched further in their understanding and practice of the Word of God and there are ways to help them in this. Do you want to plan a Bible reading promotion? Do you want to have a session with your Bible Study Group leaders to 'gee them up', so that they can gee their group members up? Is there a good biblical correspondence course that key people can do (such as the one offered by Moore College, Sydney)? Do you want to embark on a personal visit of everyone on your roll to talk over the Bible input habits they may or may not have? And how can you help people to share their insights from God's Word with each other? Do you want to plan a 'sharing time' in the public meeting, or as a regular feature of the home group program? What about a system for pairing or 'tripletting' up the congregation so that people have someone specific to talk with about what they have been learning? And on it goes.

Such public, private, and individual "speaking the truth in love" needs to be planned into the life of a church, for it provides the substructure, the strong foundation, the proper kind of maintenance for a church seeking to be 'mission minded'.

2. The Yearly Program

With the substructure of proper maintenance planned for, our attention can turn to the yearly program. What events and activities will help the congregation's mission this year?

Since people tend to be future-oriented, it is a good idea to schedule several key events that can focus the yearly program. Since we are now in mission mode, armed with our trusty piece of paper, it is fairly obvious that these key events ought to reflect our priorities. In other words, make the key events gospel events. For example, why not schedule two periods of increased evangelistic activity (I have to say 'increased' because we are now in mission mode and so evangelism ought to be on the agenda at all times)? For two consecutive weeks in both April and August you might plan to hold a guest service to which people can bring their friends, and in which there will be an opportunity for people to become Christians.

Now, how can these events provide the integration for your program? Well, for the month prior to these events your congregation will need to be inviting their friends to come, and so invitation cards/leaflets will need to be ready by then. As well as this, all of the people who attend the activities listed in your Pre-Evangelism column will be offended if they are not asked, so their 'inviters' need to be mobilised to do a lot of visits and phone calls during this month. Then there are the names on your own non-Christian contact list—be prepared for a large phone bill that month!

Since the last such event was held around the time that Noah put away his raincoat, you figure that the congregation may be a little rusty/fearful/inept at inviting people. Solution? You will hold a training session or two to walk people through their fears, the process of invitation, the importance of doing it, and to pray with them about this 'Invitation Month'.

In fact, why not get them praying as early as possible? Attendance at the monthly prayer meeting could be encouraged, since there are now some specific agenda items to pray for. The home groups could pray as a group for new contacts to invite in various places around them—that new housing district that is still not represented in church; the high school over the road; that ethnic group that is so over-represented at the shopping centre, but so under-represented in your church; their work places; that illegal casino around the corner; that sporting club; etc. Prayer cards could be issued upon which friends names could be written; pairs or triplets could regularly meet to pray through these names. You also know that there are a few people who will really take to the idea of these increased evangelism seasons, since they are already keen to share their faith with others. But you also know that they have real struggles with how to do it. With evangelism in the wind, why not invite them to do a 'How to share your faith in four easy lessons' course with you in February? They can then be given the ministry of chatting with any people who respond during the April meetings (you must expect that some will respond—God is at work, isn't he?). Some of them can then be given the opportunity to inflict the 'How to share your faith in four easy lessons' course on others before the August Increased Evangelism Season.

And don't forget to plan what will happen after these events as well. When people respond, who will be the first to contact them? They will need to have a clear diary the week immediately after the meetings. Then who will do the initial follow-up? When will these people be trained? Will you have a nurture/newcomers group? Who will lead it and how will they be trained?

February	March
• Form prayer triplets • Evangelism Training Course #1 • Invitation Training Seminar #1	• Invitation month • Two special prayer meetings
April • **Two guest services,** then • Initial visit week • Follow up/nurture group begins	**May** • Follow up/nurture group continues
June • Form prayer triplets • Evangelism Training Course #2	**July** • Invitation month • Two special prayer meetings
August • **Two guest services,** then • Initial visit week • Follow up/nurture group begins	**September** • Follow up/nurture group continues

As you can see, it doesn't take very long before your yearly program is quite full, and the beauty is that, if you allow your evangelistic events to focus the program, it is full of activities that are thoroughly mission-oriented. Once the planning is done, you could take it around to all the leaders of your groups, as well as a blank copy of your new-found handy little assessment tool, and discuss with them the function of their group and where it might fit into the church's overall vision. People love to know where they fit into the 'big picture', and this discussion will be most fruitful indeed. Then the home groups, other groups, families and individuals can also focus their prayers and activities around this program.

Planning your program also enables your public meetings to be focussed, for it provides some specifics to pray for and advertise. Can I pause on this point briefly? It seems that the advertising slot in churches is the one fixed point in their 'liturgy'; even churches that claim no liturgy will be completely liturgical about 'The Notices'. The equally ubiquitous 'Pew Bulletin' usually provides the script for the person giving 'The Notices'. It seems to me that this advertising time is often completely useless, because its importance is easily overlooked. Just setting the congregation's mission goals using your bit of paper will not mean that they will think in a mission-centred manner. The 'vision' of these biblical goals will constantly need to be put before them, so that they begin to think, breathe, walk, talk, sleep and eat these goals! Once these mission goals are enshrined in the congregation's yearly program, one way to keep the vision alive is to *advertise well.*

And what do you advertise? Often the liturgical 'Notices' spot is open slather for anyone who thrusts a notice in the hand of the minister before the service. Those days are over. The advertisements in the public meeting should reflect the vision of the congregation as a whole. So what do you advertise? You advertise the key events on your program, and you do it in an enthusiastic, positive, 'let's-all-get-amongst-it' kind of way. This strategy of advertising only the events on the congregational program will require some thought about how you will cope with things that people will invariably want to advertise. You might, for example, take a 'multi-media' approach, in which certain items (e.g. regular events, church committee, home group leaders meetings) appear in the 'bulletin' and people are trained to read this sheet for things that they are involved with. Other material that may be of interest to only some and slightly peripheral to your congregation's concerns could be put on a notice board near the morning tea area for people to browse through (e.g. the local tech wants help teaching English to migrants; there is a jobsearch seminar on; a Christian band is playing for the youth group in the neighbouring church). Then there will be other material that is of no help to your congregation, and perhaps even harmful—and why shouldn't that go straight in the round file?

What have we covered under this point? The program of events needs to be planned and it can be integrated using specifically evangelistic events. Such an integrated program can constantly focus the activities of a congregation, and, as the various groups incorporate themselves into the 'big picture', and as it is advertised well, it can keep the congregational vision in everyone's view.

3. The Pastor's Personal Program

Anyone who has a group of people under their care is a pastor to some degree, so these things are relevant to any group leader, Sunday school teacher, etc., who has to plan a program, even if I seem to be addressing *the* pastor much of the time. The difference between these kinds of pastors and *the* pastor is one of scope. It is the usual practice—and with good biblical precedent I might add—that congregations have some kind of pastor (or pastoral team) that oversees, not just a portion of the congregation, but the congregation as a whole. This role is extremely important, for the overall pastor must provide good biblical leadership for the congregation, both through his explicit teaching and through his own life. This mission-minded tool may help a pastor plan his own program as well.

It can help him care for the congregation's valuable people resource, as touched on earlier. Is each person receiving pastoral care from somebody? If they are a newcomer, who in the congregation is in touch with them? If they are an inquirer, who is answering their questions? If they are newly converted, who is following them up? If they are Christians beyond that initial stage, which Bible Study Group are they in? How are they being developed and stretched? What gifts do they have, and how can they be further trained to fulfil their ministry? In terms of their life and ministry, where do we want them to be in 12 months time? How can our congregation help to get them there?

We have also seen that it can help the pastor to plan the overall program, to understand the function of all the groups and activities, and to discuss this function with the group/activity leaders.

But it can also help organize his own personal program. Take Pastor Tom. He's been flat out for many years now in a church that has been around for many more years. And, yes, in the quietness of a dark corner somewhere, but only in the presence of (one or maybe two) friends, Tom may even admit to feeling discouraged from time to time because he feels that maybe he is in perpetual Maintenance mode. He wants to think Mission. He finds your scrappy bit of paper after you left it on the bus, and he decides to analyse *himself.*

What should he be doing? As a preacher of the gospel, and (if it is a different thing) a teacher of the Scriptures, he is someone set aside from working for a living, to devote himself to the ministry of the Word of God and to prayer. This ministry ought to be shaped by mission goals as well, shouldn't it? At the top of the left hand column he writes 'My ministry', and proceeds to list all the things that he finds himself engaged in during a normal month of ministry. Then he takes a big breath and takes a long look at the result:

	EVANGELISM				EDIFICATION			SUPPORT TO MINISTRY
My ministry: Actual Tom	Raising Awareness	Initial Contact	Pre-Evangelism	Evangelism	Follow-up	Nurture	Training in Ministry	
Sunday Service + preaching								
Scripture Teaching								
Committees (x4)								
Organize rosters								
Bible Study (x1)								
Baptism inquirers (phone)								
Marriages								
Funerals								
Hospital visits (congregation + non)								
Men's night								

He decides that his new mission-centred mind doesn't like everything he sees on the paper. He grabs a fresh piece, and writes the heading 'My ideal ministry' and proceeds to list the things he would like to be involved in, now that his ministry is mission.

What should he do? Well, he remembers that he is first and foremost a gospel preacher—at least in theory. That is what he has been trained for, and that is what his church has commissioned him for. He is the one who doesn't have to support himself, in order that he can be free to devote himself to prayer and the ministry of the Word of God. So he had better do that with all his energy! He has always put a high status on his preaching, and prepares his sermons very well. But have they been mission focussed? Come to think of it, there have been more than enough topical sermons—he finds it easier to say what's on his heart, than to do the hard work of preparing an unfamiliar passage from Zechariah! He decides to commit himself to expository sermons, so that his preaching ministry will be shaped by God's agenda, not his. And then there is the focus of his sermons. He admits to himself that he very rarely directs his sermons to people as people; he tends to always talk as if everyone in church is a Christian, and fairly keen about it. Perhaps he needs to have more awareness of the variety of people listening to him, and cast a wider net in his preaching. Maybe he should try to preach what God's word says to anyone and everyone who lives in this messed-up world. That would make it much easier for his congregation to bring anyone they know along to church whenever the opportunity presented itself, and they would be guaranteed of hearing something relevant.

	EVANGELISM				EDIFICATION			SUPPORT TO MINISTRY
My ministry: Actual Tom	Raising Awareness	Initial Contact	Pre-Evangelism	Evangelism	Follow-up	Nurture	Training in Ministry	
Expository preaching, focused widely								

What else should he do? He looks at the Evangelism column, and it is a sorry sight indeed. He's never really felt all that gifted in the area—he is 'more of a teacher than an evangelist'. But, he thinks, Paul could say "imitate me as I imitate Christ", and he was talking about taking the gospel to people to get them saved (1 Cor 11:1). And he could tell Timothy —poor old timid Timothy—to "do the work of an evangelist", which probably indicates that he didn't see himself as an evangelist but had to do the work anyway (2 Tim 4:5)! And besides, if the pastor is never seen evangelizing, how will the congregation follow his model? Well, they will—they won't evangelize either!

Our very self-analytic Tom continues to think, deep down: *I don't want to evangelize, because it fills me with fear.* But then, isn't everyone fearful? Even Paul sometimes felt the pressure and "despaired even of life" (2 Cor 1:8), and he had to ask for prayer that he would be more bold (Eph 6:19-20). It seems that he presented a model not of someone who had it all together as an evangelist, but of someone who was just as likely to go to jelly as the next man! But that was his point, for he was an example of someone whose weakness was his strength, because in his weakness it was very clear that any 'success' was God's work, not his (2 Cor 1:8-11; 11:16-12:11, and 1 Cor 2:1-5).

Tom suddenly realises that in all his fearful reluctance to evangelize he suddenly becomes the perfect model of an evangelist. He can model how to keep taking the opportunities God provides *despite his fear* ; how to fail *and get up again for more;* how to have a priceless treasure in an old cracked cup (2 Cor 4:7-12); how to be only and always a beggar, but one who can point others to where they can find bread. Tom suddenly realises that the only criterion for doing the work of an evangelist is not ability or temperament or strength of desire to do it—the only criterion is that we have believed a message about God's overwhelming grace that wants to spread to more and more people (2 Cor 4:13-15). "I believed; therefore I have spoken", says Paul. And Tom resolves to say the same thing from now on, with God's help. His mind is racing: "My evangelistic edge needs to be constantly modelled in *public* (Do my sermons say something to the insider and the outsider?), in *private* (Do our prayer meetings and home group pray for people's conversion? Why doesn't my home group have the occasional dialogue meeting where non-Christian friends can come to hear the gospel and have their questions answered?), and with *individuals* (I could ask people how and when they were converted? I could seriously try to turn conversations to the gospel more often? I should expect people to become Christians, show them how, invite them to do so and offer to pray with them on the spot)". It seems that from now on, our Tom is planning to model evangelism.

What else should he do? Ephesians 4:11-12 and 2 Timothy 2:2 come to his mind, and it dawns on him that he has a unique responsibility and opportunity to train his congregation for their various ministries in the body of Christ. He should be training people. That column needs to be chock-a-block for this pastor! As he prays for people he should be asking for the wisdom to discern their gifts and the opportunity to push them ahead in their Christian life and ministry. He can think of a ready made opportunity for training straight away. Although he hasn't been taking advantage of them as much as he should, he suddenly realises that he probably has many more opportunities to take the gospel to people than anyone he knows, simply by virtue of being the pastor. Why doesn't he plan to always take people with him when he visits or teaches scripture or preaches as a guest somewhere else, so that they can watch him share the gospel? Then, after they have watched, they can try themselves, and he can watch them and give them feedback. Then, when they are ready for it, they could take someone else with them into their gospel opportunities and train them, and he could train them how to train them. If enough people were doing it, perhaps they could arrange to go on evangelistic visits for one particular night each week. They could all meet for prayer and a bit of input, and then go off to share the gospel on their visits. Then there are other training opportunities, such as running courses, all the regular meetings, special leaders meetings and so on. This has really got him thinking! He finishes writing out his 'Ideal Tom' sheet. (See page 69)

Of course, life is never ideal, and there are a few things he sees on the list that he would rather not see on it (labelled with an asterisk), but until he can get rid of them elsewhere, he'll keep them on for the time being. But simply by doing this exercise, he has now been made aware of an area that he will 'peel off' as soon as someone else comes along who is more eminently suited to that area than he is.

And, of course, the next thing he will need to do is to plan his own personal program. Each week his schedule needs to reflect his priorities. He needs to fill in the blanks according to his mission goals, rather than waiting for others to fill in the blanks for him. And, once again, he needs to have some flexibility, for things do 'come up' that may be worthwhile in the long run (after all, God is ultimately in charge of our time, not us)—so why not plan some 'slush time' that can be filled if and when it is needed. The asterisked items may also find a place on the weekly timetable, but their fate is hanging in the balance now that their true worth has been evaluated!

A lot more could no doubt be said, but we have to stop talking somewhere. This tool needs to prove its usefulness as we begin to use it in our real-life setting.

One last comment remains, and then it is over to you.

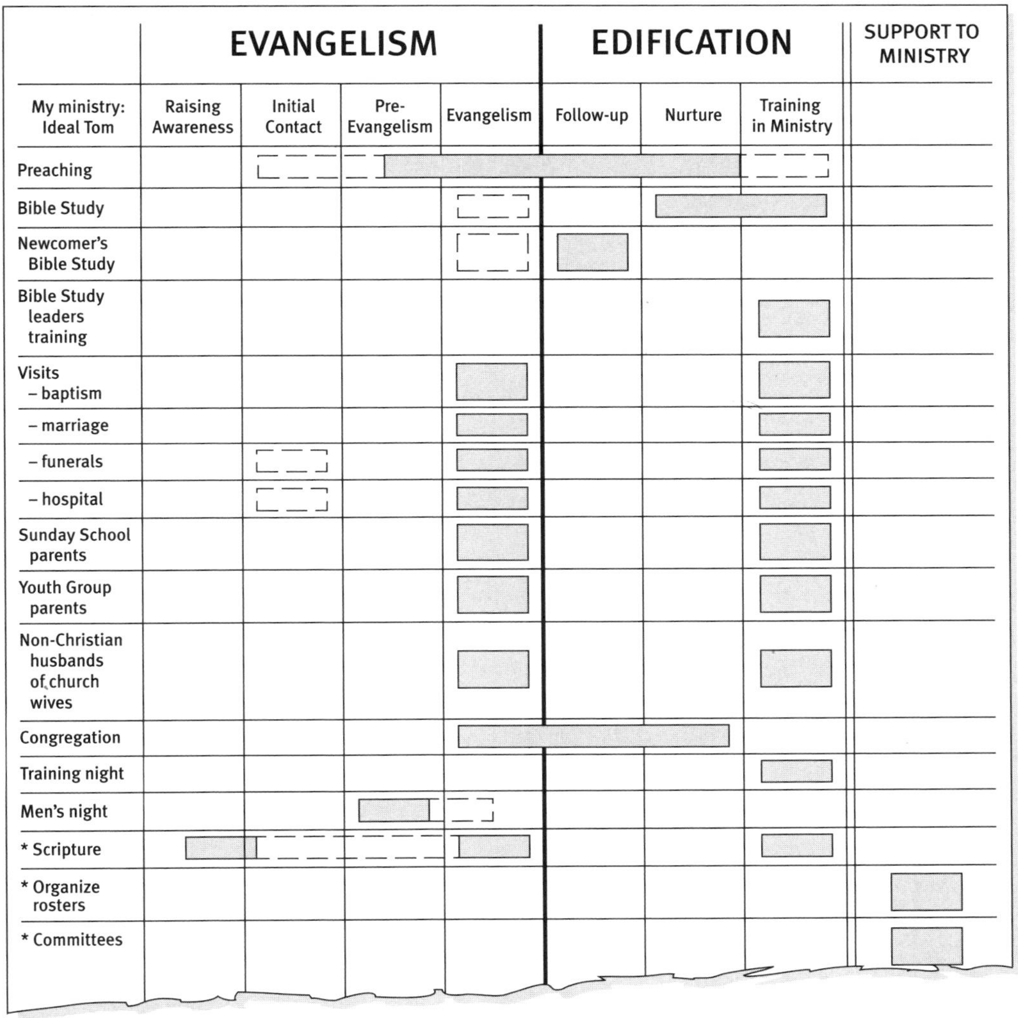

	EVANGELISM				EDIFICATION			SUPPORT TO MINISTRY
My ministry: Ideal Tom	Raising Awareness	Initial Contact	Pre-Evangelism	Evangelism	Follow-up	Nurture	Training in Ministry	
Preaching								
Bible Study								
Newcomer's Bible Study								
Bible Study leaders training								
Visits – baptism								
– marriage								
– funerals								
– hospital								
Sunday School parents								
Youth Group parents								
Non-Christian husbands of church wives								
Congregation								
Training night								
Men's night								
* Scripture								
* Organize rosters								
* Committees								

Chapter 9

Over to you

So now you have it. A tool that is simple but extremely versatile. It enables anyone to become mission minded—to centre their ministry on mission. Perhaps some more specific objectives need to be filled in alongside these general, biblical goals, but nevertheless the mission goals discussed here will go a long way towards keeping the Mafia from your door! But, far more importantly, these goals will go a long way towards helping establish a mission-centred ministry, and this will help to bring the gospel to a lost world. If they manage to get us out of a maintenance rut, and so help others find their way into heaven, then it is worth the hard work of thinking, analysing, planning and implementing them, isn't it? What a great thought that is!

We have many good intentions, yet often they aren't enough to enable the exercise of a planned, purposeful and strategic ministry. Perhaps this simple tool on a now crumpled piece of rectangular paper will help us get involved and stay involved in Christ's all-important mission to seek and to save the lost. I pray that it does at least that. But now, it's over to you.

Appendix 1

The Mission Minded Tool

Overleaf is a copy of the *Mission Minded* tool that can be photocopied for your convenience.

	EVANGELISM				EDIFICATION			SUPPORT TO MINISTRY
	Raising Awareness	Initial Contact	Pre-Evangelism	Evangelism	Follow-up	Nurture	Training in Ministry	

a 'mission minded' publishing company

In many ways, what makes Matthias Media different from many other Christian publishers is that we wholeheartedly believe in the principles outlined in *Mission Minded.* We believe that our job is not just to pump out entertaining Christian books (what you might call 'publishing maintenance mode'); our goal is to provide resources for Christians who want to join in Christ's mission.

In practical terms, this means that we have worked at building a range of resources that span across the mission goals Peter Bolt outlines in *Mission Minded*, and particularly in the fundamental categories of evangelism, follow-up, nurture and training in ministry.

Opposite is a selection of our resources, analysed the 'Mission Minded' way.

For a full description of these resources, and for the many other resources not listed here, contact us for a free copy of our annual Resource Guide, or visit our website to browse the online catalogue.

1800 814 360
or in Sydney:
(02) 9663 1478

Reply Paid 225,
Kingsford
NSW 2032

FAX
(02) 9663 3265
(pay by credit card or invoice)

EMAIL
info@matthiasmedia.com.au

INTERNET
www.matthiasmedia.com.au

	EVANGELISM		EDIFICATION		
Matthias Media Resources	Pre-Evangelism	Evangelism	Follow-up	Nurture	Training in Ministry
Bible studies – Bible studies on different books of the Bible and topics, including video-based studies				■	
– Just for Starters (7 Basic Bible studies)			■		
– Simply Christianity (Enquirers course)		■			
Tracts – 2 Ways to Live: the choice we all face		■			
– 2 Ways to Live: Multimedia CD-Rom		■			
Books – Simply Christianity: Beyond Religion (by John Dickson)		■		□	
– The True and Living God (by Kim Hawtrey)		□		■	
– Kicking-Off (by Al Stewart and Ed Vaughan)			■		
– Setting Hearts on Fire: A guide to giving evangelistic talks (by John Chapman)					■
– Unnatural Enemies: Science and Christianity (by Kirsten Birkett)	■			■	
Training – Six Steps to Encouragement: training all Christians to encourage others with God's word					■
– 2 Ways to Live: Know the Gospel, share the Gospel					■